THE HOUSE THAT SHE BUILT

To Zachary, Zoey, Quentin, and the future generations of skilled workers and business owners in residential construction.

Text © 2021 by Mollie Elkman
Illustrations © 2021 by Georgia Castellano

ISBN: 978-0-86718-785-4
eISBN: 978-0-86718-786-1

Printed in Italy

25 24 22 21   2 3 4 5

Patricia Potts, Senior Director, Publishing • Jerry Howard, CEO
John McGeary, Senior Vice President, Business Development and Brand Strategy
Denise Miller, Vice President, Event Product & Brand Marketing

NAHB BuilderBooks
1201 15th Street NW, Washington, DC 20005
BuilderBooks.com

Let's explore 18 different
skilled jobs needed to build a home!

Architect	Engineer	General Contractor
Excavator	Concrete Laborer	Framer
Electrician	Plumber	HVAC Technician
Roofer	Insulation Contractor	Drywaller
Cabinet Manufacturer	Finish Carpenter	Tiler
Painter	Interior Designer	Landscaper

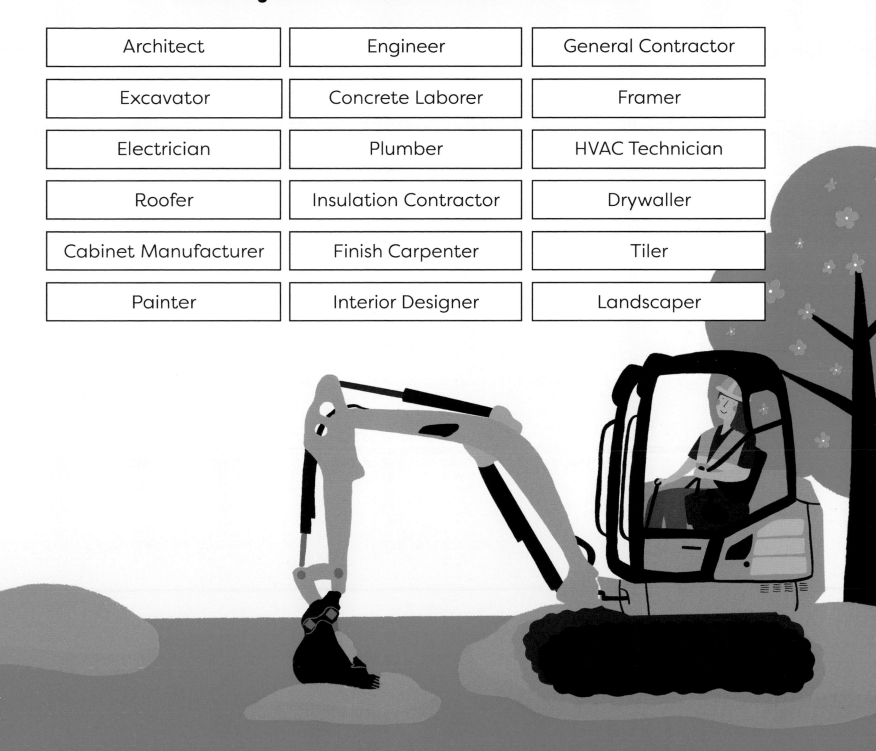

these are tiny little notes that the
architect might make about her draft

PLANS FOR THE HOUSE THAT SHE BUILT

This is the woman who created the design.

The Architect uses science and art to draw the building plans.

This is the house that she built.

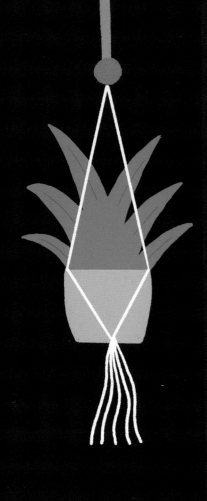

This is the woman who engineered the structure.

The Engineer does calculations to make sure the structure is strong and safe.

This is the house that she built.

This is the woman who managed the project.

The General Contractor oversees construction, materials, and timelines.

This is the house that she built.

This is the woman who excavated the land.

The Excavator prepares the land by clearing, digging, and evening it out.

This is the house that she built.

This is the woman who poured the foundation.

The Concrete Laborer mixes, pours, and smooths out the concrete.

This is the house that she built.

This is the woman who assembled the framing.

The Framer measures, cuts, and puts together the wood pieces.

This is the house that she built.

This is the woman who installed the electrical wires.

The Electrician connects the wiring that controls the lighting, computers, and TV.

This is the house that she built.

This is the woman who installed the plumbing.

The Plumber installs the pipes and water lines for running water and flushing toilets.

This is the house that she built.

This is the woman who installed the mechanical lines.

The HVAC Technician installs the systems for heating, ventilation, and air conditioning.

This is the house that she built.

**This is the woman
who laid the roof.**

The Roofer installs the
roof using materials to
make it strong and
waterproof.

**This is the house
that she built.**

This is the woman who installed the insulation.

The Insulation Contractor makes sure the house will be at the right temperature year-round.

This is the house that she built.

This is the woman who hung the drywall.

The Drywaller cuts and hangs the panels that make the walls.

This is the house that she built.

This is the woman who built the cabinets.

The Cabinet Manufacturer measures, cuts, and builds the cabinets to fit perfectly.

This is the house that she built.

This is the woman who installed the trim.

The Finish Carpenter works with wood to create and install doors, trims, and shelves.

This is the house that she built.

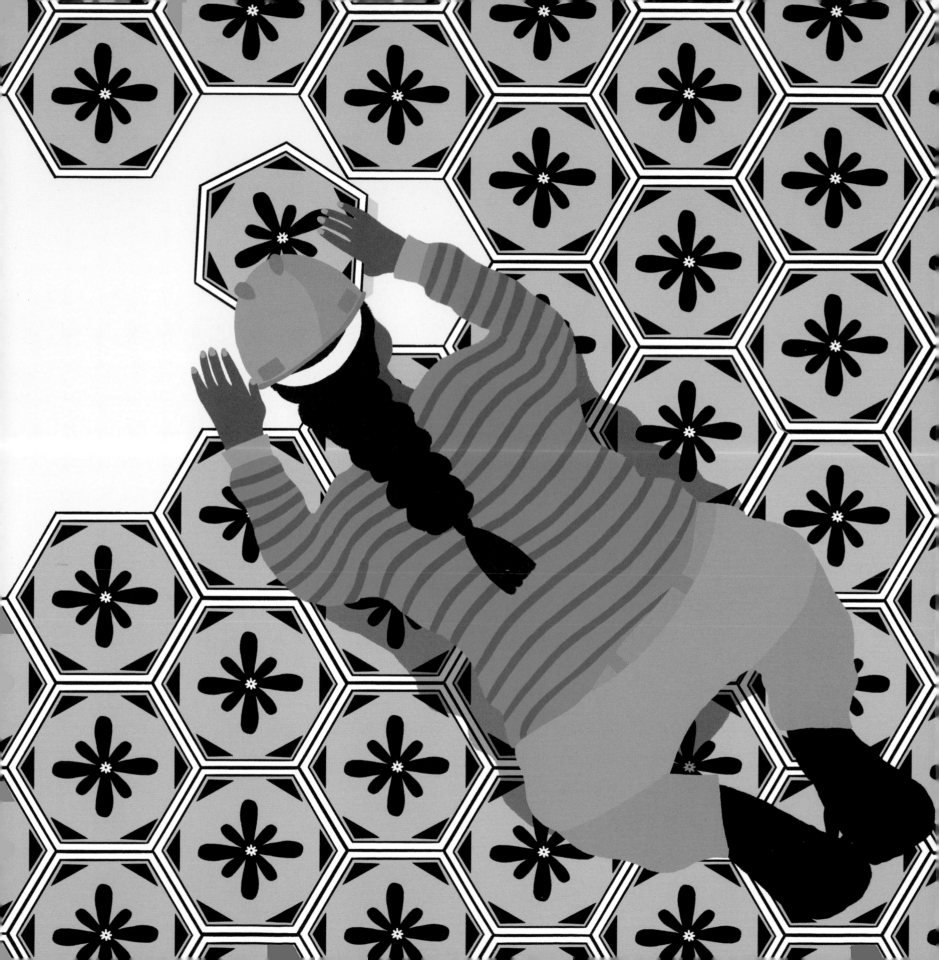

**This is the woman who
laid the tile.**

The Tiler places and secures the
tiles that protect and decorate
walls and floors.

This is the house that she built.

This is the woman who painted the walls.

The Painter applies the paint that covers and colors the walls inside and out.

This is the house that she built.

This is the woman who selected the finishes and furnishings.

The Interior Designer creates the look of the rooms with furniture, decorations, art, and color.

This is the house that she built.

This is the woman who perfected the landscaping.

The Landscaper designs, builds, and plants to make the outdoor space special.

This is the house that she built.

These are the women who
are proud to say "this house is for sale!"
after perfecting the landscaping,
selecting the finishes and furnishings,
painting the walls, laying the tile,
installing the trim, building the cabinets,
hanging the drywall, installing the insulation,

laying the roof,
installing the electric, plumbing, and mechanical lines,
assembling the framing, building the foundation,
excavating the land, managing the project,
engineering the structure, and creating the design.

This is the house that she built.

Let's talk about your skills!

Can you count the number of women in the book?

Counting is math. Many of the
skills in this book use math!

Do you have a favorite color in the book?

Creativity and art are part of the many
skills that go into building a home.

**Have you ever made a house out of building blocks
or built a fort out of blankets and pillows?**

Building with your hands is so much fun!

SheBuiltBook.com